VENUS AND SERENA

WILLIAMS

VENUS AND SERENA
WILLIAMS

GABRIEL FLYNN
THE CHILD'S WORLD®, INC.

ON THE COVER...

Front cover: Venus (left) watches her sister Serena (right) during the winners' ceremony after the 1999 International Tennis Grand Slam Cup.
Page 2: Serena (left) and Venus (right) share a laugh during their first-round doubles match at the 1999 French Open.

Copyright © 2001 by The Child's World®, Inc.
All rights reserved. No part of this book may be
reproduced or utilized in any form or by any means
without written permission from the publisher.
Printed in the United States of America.

Library of Congress Cataloging-in-Publication Data
Flynn, Gabriel.
Venus and Serena Williams / by Gabriel Flynn.
p. cm.
Includes index.
ISBN 1-56766-834-8 (lib. reinforced. : alk. paper)
1. Williams, Venus, 1980—Juvenile literature.
2. Williams, Serena, 1981—Juvenile literature.
3. Tennis players—United States—Biography—Juvenile literature.
4. Afro-American women tennis players—Biography—Juvenile literature.
[1. Williams, Venus, 1980– 2. Williams, Serena, 1981–
3. Tennis players. 4. Afro-Americans—Biography. 5. Women—Biography.]   I. Title.
GV994.A1 F58 2000
796.342'092'273—dc21
[B]   00-029039

PHOTO CREDITS

© AP/Wide World Photos: cover, 2, 6, 9, 10, 13, 15, 16, 19, 22
© Bongarts Photography./SportsChrome-USA: 20

TABLE OF CONTENTS

SISTERS

It's the mid-1980s in the **ghetto** of Compton, California, just south of Los Angeles. Life is hard. Garbage and broken glass lie in the streets. Crime is high, and buildings are covered with spray-painted **graffiti.** In the middle of this city are run-down tennis courts. The fences are rusty, the courts are cracked, and the nets need repair. Does anybody even use these courts?

"Whoosh" goes the ball as one family plays. This is the Williams family: a dad, a mom, and five daughters. The two youngest daughters are Venus and Serena. They show the most interest and play every chance they can.

HOW THEY GOT STARTED

How did the Williams family get interested in tennis? Richard, the father, says he was watching a tournament on TV and saw the champion get a check for a lot of money. He told his wife, Oracene, "Let's put our kids in tennis so they can become millionaires." And that's what they did. Throughout Venus's and Serena's childhood, their parents were their coaches. This was very unusual. Not only had their parents never coached, they didn't even know how to play tennis!

Serena (left) and Venus (right) playing during a doubles match in the Italian Open on May 7, 1998.

Many people said that someone else should have been their coach. But famous tennis coach Nick Bolletteiri disagrees. He says, "The road they've gone on couldn't have been better selected. . . . Nobody knows those girls better than their parents."

Venus and Serena began playing in the United States Tennis Association (USTA) for kids. They were the best players in their area. By age 10, Venus had already won 30 titles and was **ranked** number one in the 10–12 age group.

Although Venus and Serena were very good, they didn't play in as many tournaments as most other girls. Their parents wanted them to focus on school.

CHANGING COACHES

When Venus was 11 and Serena was 10, the Williams family moved to Palm Beach Gardens, Florida. There they could play against better competition. Their house had a tennis court in the backyard. The sisters also began training with professional tennis coach Richard Macci. He said that Venus was so competitive, she would "run over broken glass to hit a ball." His practice schedule was very hard. The girls practiced six hours a day, six days a week. They also had to hit 200 serves every day.

Venus returns a shot to Ai Sugiyama of Japan during their match at the Evert Cup on March 9, 1997.

After a year and a half, Richard decided that he and Oracene should coach the girls again. Many people thought this was a bad decision, but not Macci. He said Richard "has done what he thought in his heart was best for his girls." Would the sisters make it in professional tennis being coached by their parents? The world was waiting to see.

A BIG SPLASH ON THE PROFESSIONAL TOUR

Venus and Serena are **African American,** and there are very few African American professional tennis players. The two are lively and shout and jump a lot on the court. When they play, they wear bright clothes and colorful beads in their hair. "Me and Serena are a whole different thing happening," said Venus. Venus is the taller, faster player. Her best shots are her serve and her overhead smash. Serena is shorter and has a more muscular body. She wins with her powerful backhand. Both sisters are very strong.

Just how strong are they? At Wimbledon in 1998, Venus slammed a serve at 125 miles per hour. It was the fastest serve by a woman ever! Then, in the 1998 European Championships, she played Mary Pierce. "Wham!" She broke her own world record with a serve at 127 miles per hour! Venus said, "I've just turned 18 so I'm just going to get stronger. . . . In the last year, I gained 9 miles per hour on my serve." Serena's fastest serve was 112 miles per hour.

← Venus slams a powerful serve against Martina Hingis during their match at the Evert Cup on March 13, 1998.

THE U.S. OPEN

In 1997, Venus played in the U.S. Open. This important tournament was played in the brand-new Arthur Ashe Stadium in Flushing Meadow, New York. The stadium was named after Arthur Ashe, the most famous African American tennis player of all time. Venus wanted to play in the U.S. Open to show that other African Americans can be good at tennis. Venus said, "I think with this moment in the first year in Arthur Ashe Stadium, it all represents everyone being together, everyone having a chance to play."

She was **unseeded,** which means she was supposed to be one of the worst players in the tournament. But she played well and surprised the other players. She won all her matches and made it to the championship match.

In the championship, she played the world's top-ranked player, Martina Hingis. Venus played hard but lost. Although she lost, she made history. She was the first unseeded player ever to reach the finals. She was also the first African American woman to reach the finals since 1958! The world began to see that Venus was going to be a top player.

Venus follows through on a serve from Larisa Neiland of Latvia at the U.S. Open on August 25, 1997.

MOVING UP

In 1997, Serena was ranked 453rd in the world. Only eight months later, she had risen to Number 20. With her powerful backhand, she played well in seven tournaments. One of those was in Sydney, Australia. There she beat the world's Number 2–ranked player, Lindsay Davenport.

Although she earned her high ranking by using her talents, Serena gave the credit to her dad's coaching. She said, "If it wasn't for my dad, I definitely wouldn't be here today. He always keeps my confidence up."

Venus also moved up in the rankings. Her father taught her to keep using her strong serve and overhead smash. She said, "All my career I've had people ask when I was going to get a real coach. . . . Now, hopefully, people see that our parents knew what they were doing."

Serena returns a ball to Australia's Nicole Pratt during the U.S. Open on August 31, 1998.

→

THE LIPTON CHAMPIONSHIPS

In 1998, both Venus and Serena played in the Lipton Championships in Oklahoma City, Oklahoma. Serena was unseeded, but she amazed the tennis world by beating three players in a row. She then had to play Martina Hingis, the top-ranked player in the world. It was a tough match, and Serena lost in a tiebreaker. Although she was knocked out of the tournament, she was finally recognized as one of the best new players. Her world ranking soared. But what about Venus?

Venus was also playing well. She won her first four matches without losing a **set,** which is a group of games in a tennis match. Now it was her turn to play Hingis. It took three sets, but Venus won. She beat the best player in the world!

She now was in the championship match against Anna Kournikova. It was a tough match that also took three sets. Venus lost the first set, but she began to play better and won the second set. Serena and her mother cheered her on. The final set took only 26 minutes. With her powerful serve, Venus won that set, too!

Venus was now ranked Number 10. Only one other player had ever moved up so quickly in the computer rankings. But when Venus accepted her trophy, she wasn't thinking of her ranking. She was thinking of her family. She said, "When I win, everyone wins. . . . It helps Serena . . . because when I win, I can tell her what I did to win."

Venus smiles as she holds the Lipton Championship trophy after beating Anna Kournikova on March 28, 1998.

REACHING HIGHER AND HIGHER

Venus and Serena kept climbing in the world rankings. In early 1999, they were both ranked in the top 10. Early in the season, Venus and Serena took the tennis world by storm. Serena won her first singles title at the Paris Open, and Venus won the IGA Classic on the same day! They became the first sisters ever to win tournaments on the same day. Then, two weeks later, Serena won her second tournament in a row, the Evert Cup.

On March 28, Venus and Serena met in the championship match of the Lipton Championships. It was the first time they had played each other for a tournament title. In fact, it was the first time in 115 years that any sisters had faced each other for a title. It was a tough, hard-fought match, with each sister winning one of the first two sets. Then, Venus won the final set 6–4 to win the championship. But Serena wasn't sad. She said, "I definitely look forward to another final with Venus. It's what we always dreamed of."

RETURN TO THE U.S. OPEN

In 1999, Venus and Serena returned to Arthur Ashe Stadium to play in the U.S. Open. Martina Hingis was again the top-ranked player. Could the Williams sisters defeat Hingis and win the tournament this year?

Serena (left) and Venus (right) hold up their trophies after the Lipton Championships on March 28, 1999.

Venus and Serena were playing well. Venus played Hingis in the semifinals. Hingis won the first set 6–1, but Venus won the second 6–4. In the final set, Venus lost 6–3. She was heartbroken. Serena played the Number 2–ranked player, Lindsay Davenport. Serena won 6–4, 1–6, 6–4. Serena advanced to the finals to play Hingis.

Serena wasn't afraid. She served well and overpowered Hingis, winning 6–3, 7–6. She won the U.S. Open! At age 17, she was one of the few African Americans to win a major championship. Serena said, "It's just too exciting to compute right now." Her win was such a major accomplishment, Serena even got a call from President Bill Clinton.

But the Williams sisters weren't finished yet. In doubles, they advanced to the finals. In the championship match, they teamed up against Chanda Rubin and Sandrine Testud—and won. They had swept the U.S. Open in singles and doubles!

HEADING FOR THE FUTURE

Going into 2000, Venus was ranked Number 3 in the world and Serena was ranked Number 4. Their goal is to be the top two players in the rankings. By believing in each other, Venus and Serena just might reach their goal. Watch out, world, here come the Williams sisters!

Serena returns the ball during a match at the 1999 U.S. Open.

TIMELINE

VENUS

June 17, 1980	Venus Williams is born in Lynwood, California.
March 28, 1998	Venus defeats Serena in the title match to win the Lipton Championships in singles.
October 4, 1998	Venus wins the Grand Slam Cup in singles.
May 1999	Venus wins the Italian Open in singles.
June 1999	Venus wins the French Open in doubles with Serena.
August 1999	Venus wins the New Haven Open in singles.
September 12, 1999	Venus wins the U.S. Open in doubles.
July 8, 2000	Venus wins the Wimbledon women's singles title.
July 10, 2000	Venus wins the Wimbledon women's doubles title with Serena.

SERENA

September 26, 1981	Serena Williams is born in Saginaw, Michigan.
March 1, 1998	Serena wins the IGA Tennis Classic in doubles with Venus.
February 28, 1999	Serena wins the Paris Open in singles.
June 1999	Serena wins the French Open in doubles with Venus.
September 11, 1999	Serena wins the U.S. Open in singles.
September 12, 1999	Serena wins the U.S. Open in doubles with Venus.
February 20, 2000	Serena wins the Faber Grand Prix in singles.
July 10, 2000	Serena wins the Wimbledon women's doubles title with Venus.

Venus (left) and Serena (right) chat during their doubles final at the 1999 U.S. Open.

GLOSSARY

African American (AF–rih–kan uh–MAYR–ih–kan)
An African American is a black American whose ancestors came from Africa. Venus and Serena are African Americans.

ghetto (GEH–toh)
A ghetto is a section of a city where minority groups live often because of social pressures. The Williams family lived in a ghetto in Compton, California.

graffiti (gruh–FEE–tee)
Words or pictures painted on walls are called graffiti. In the 1980s, Los Angeles had lots of spray-painted graffiti.

ranked (RANKT)
When an athlete is ranked, he or she is given a number. The lower the number, the better the player is. Venus and Serena want to be ranked Number 1 and Number 2 in the world.

set (SET)
A set is a group of games. In women's tennis, the first player to win two sets wins the match.

unseeded (un–SEE–ded)
A seed is a rank for the top players in a tournament. When Venus and Serena were starting out, they were unseeded because they weren't expected to win.

INDEX